This Journal Belongs to:

Name ....

Email ....

Telephone ....

Breathe

Escape

JOURNAL

STERLING
New York

Escape

Get on top of your emails, spend more time with family, eat well, clean the house, nurture relationships—it seems there's always something that needs doing, always someone who needs your attention. If only there was time in the day to devote to doing something for yourself, you'd jump at the chance, wouldn't you?

Allowing ourselves to slow down can be a challenge. A negative inner commentary can insist if you're not accomplishing something, you're wasting time. Success today is synonomous with being busy. If no one's around, you'll reach for the to-do list, pick up the phone, take out the trash—anything to avoid claiming a moment to rest and relax, or engage in an activity that brings you joy.

But that can change. Brought to you by the creators of *Breathe* magazine, this journal is your chance to carve out a little solitude, some time alone to go inward, steady the mind, and simply be. Beautifully illustrated, it's filled with restorative exercises and prompts for reflection and personal growth. Use it to build a new relationship with someone who deserves your attention—you.

Breathe

breathemagazine.com

Contents

> "I only went out for a walk and finally concluded to stay out 'till sundown, for going out, I found, was really going in."

John Muir

A World in a Grain of Sand

Come rain or shine, a walk along the seashore is a great way to reconnect with the inner self and find peace in a chaotic world.

Picture the scene: You step down from the concrete steps and onto firm, white sand. You can feel the gritty texture through the sole of your shoe. You walk forward, slowly, allowing each footfall to place distance between you and the world of emails, phone calls, and the constant news stream that you left behind when you shut the front door this morning. Each and every step takes you toward the sound of the sea—the rhythmic, heavy drag of the sand, the seagull's keening cry, its slender shape falling across your eyeline . . .

Before long, you are a million mindful miles away from the busy life you entered when you woke up and started scrolling through email and social media. You are stepping away from the onslaught of unsettling news stories, crime, unkindness, fear, the fake rendition of success, the wave of supposedly perfect families doing perfect family things in perfectly clean houses and exotic locations.

The clatter of your world begins to recede. In its place you begin to focus on the beach beneath your feet—small stones, shells, fossils. You slow your pace, focused and aware. You are fully in this moment. There is nothing but the sounds of the sea and the simple beauty of small things.

Look Back in Joy

The seaside means different things to different people. Walk along many a beach nowadays and you're as likely to see windsurfers, bodyboarders, canoeists, and yogis practicing downward-facing dog as you are dog walkers throwing sticks for excited canines to retrieve.

Whatever the reason for going there, the sea's smells and sounds invariably evoke powerful memories and elicit strong emotional responses. The scrape of a bucket and spade on the sand; the smell of lobster rolls and the sweet taste of ice cream; the jumbled, jingling music of arcades and slot machines. All bring back memories. For many, these will be of happy, relaxed family days, enjoying the sense of freedom vactations bring. And memories are powerful—a positive recollection is like a touchstone to emotional peace. It's one of the reasons why being near the sea can benefit well-being.

Take a Mindful Moment

A stroll along the beach can provide a natural antidote to stress—the clear, unobstructed light lends positivity to one's mood. And consciously practicing mindfulness as you walk can make it all the more powerful. It needn't be a strenuous or ritualized route. It's about being mindful and noticing your surroundings, with the negative inner commentary switched off. This will enable body and mind to be fully aware of the environment, without judging it.

Beachcombing is a good example. Several things happen when a person purposefully combs the beach for objects: a physical slowing down of the body and a focused gaze on the small things—pebbles, fossils, shells, and discarded objects that would otherwise go unnoticed. The change of perspective is almost unspoken. The message? Even tiny things are beautiful in their own right. By focusing the mind on this idea and physically responding to it, the beachcomber enjoys a natural spell of mindfulness.

You can reap the benefits of a trip to the seaside just by sitting close to hear the sounds of the seashore. Simply quiet the inner voice, allowing the soundscape to wash over your mind. When you leave, "take" the sea with you—store its sounds, smells, images, and lightness in your mind. And when anxiety strikes—the constant striving and comparison that is part of the modern psyche—revisit this inner sea and find your own seaside calm in the chaos of life.

"The sea, once it casts its spell, holds one in its net of wonder forever."

Jacques-Yves Cousteau

SEASIDE SLOWDOWNS

Here are some easy ways to practice mindfulness on the beach, or anywhere you can hear the sounds of the sea. Each of the exercises should be performed for around 10 minutes (or whatever you're in the mood for). After each exercise, reflect on your experience in the provided space. Refer back to these positive memories whenever you want to lift your mood.

Beach Bench Meditation
Find a place to sit where you can hear the sounds of the sea. A bench is perfect, but a big rock, a beach blanket, or even just sitting in your car seat with the windows down will do. Place both feet flat on the ground and make sure you're comfortable. You don't have to close your eyes, but it can help to eliminate any distractions. Allow the sounds around you to drift into your mind. Every time your inner voice pipes up, imagine it blowing away on a sea breeze.

....

....

....

....

Sea-rhythm Breathing
Sit comfortably, as above. Listen to the rhythm of the sea. Breathe in and out, echoing the ebb and flow of the water. Focus on your breathing, matching it to the sea. It should be roughly a count of six on the inhale and the same on the exhale. As you're breathing, allow the thoughts and experiences of your day to rise up through you and imagine the waves carrying them out to sea.

....

....

....

....

....

Found-object Focus

Allow yourself to be drawn to an object. It could be a pebble, a shell, or piece of driftwood. It might even be a building, rock, or tree. Allow your focus to rest gently on the object. Look at it as if for the first time and visually explore its every facet. Imagine the object in the world and then being part of the world. Then think of yourself being in the world and being part of the world.

....

....

....

....

Walking Meditation

Begin walking along the beach. Remind yourself there is no destination and that walking is the point. Slow your pace down so that it becomes deliberate—each movement an act of focus. Allow yourself to become immersed in the movement, focusing entirely on the physical sensations.

....

....

....

....

Touch Point

Once on the seashore, remove your shoes. Put both feet on the sand or shingle and concentrate on how the surface feels on the soles, the part of you that is physically grounded in the world. Think about the texture—is it smooth or sharp, warm or cool, light or heavy? Close your eyes and, if it's safe to do so, immerse yourself in the feeling—wiggle your toes under the shingle or pebbles, if need be. Then enjoy the memories and images it evokes.

....

....

....

....

Silent Cities

There's a quiet side to urban areas. Secluded courtyards, small cafés, and hidden gardens invite reflection and the chance to unwind, slow down, and even create. You just need to find them.

Most people need quiet, though how much will be different for everyone. Quietness can be experienced sitting in a park, taking a lunchtime walk, or spending time alone in a museum. Regardless of where and how you like to spend this downtime, one thing is certain—it can be a struggle to find it. On a daily basis, there's an unwelcome cacophony of sound, from the frenetic rush of city traffic to the incessant ringtones of cell phones. While much of this noise is fleeting, the accumulative effects aren't.

Shush, Please!
So adverse is noise pollution that in 2011 the World Health Organization calculated its cost. It reported that more than one million healthy years are taken off Europe's collective life expectancy annually, with the effects including sleep loss, heart disease, stroke, prolonged stress, and even delayed reading and comprehension in children. With the human body continuing to respond to sound even when it is asleep, according to the United Kingdom's National Sleep Foundation, is it any wonder you can find yourself craving peace and quiet?

Meditation, walking, and practicing mindfulness can help. In fact, quietness is necessary for renewed productivity and creativity, according to psychologist Ferris Jabr. It offers respite from daily to-do lists and overwhelming schedules, making it possible to be in the moment, uninterrupted.

As essayist Tim Kreider shares in his article "The 'Busy' Trap," idleness is the means to a more fulfilled life—that contrary to self-imposed busyness, a slower life is not one where every minute is accounted for, but where dreams and imaginations flourish. He writes: "The space and quiet that idleness provides is a necessary condition for standing back from life and seeing it whole, for making unexpected connections and waiting for the wild summer lightning strikes of inspiration—it is, paradoxically, necessary to getting any work done."

Finding Quiet Places

Public parks and gardens immediately come to mind as do museums, libraries, and even bookstores in their quieter hours. In fact, there are a multitude of places, as author Siobhan Wall found when she started researching her books dedicated to this very subject. "I sought out galleries I'd always thought might show intriguing work but had never visited, and wandered down small streets with inviting shops, quickly leaving if they played music and lingering for a while if they didn't. I found this was the best way to discover many places—just to walk around."

Taking inspiration from the writings of French philosopher Guy Debord, Siobhan allowed herself the time to wander aimlessly. In doing so, she found more than 140 quiet spots. By abandoning regular routines, discarding city maps, and finding the time, it is possible to discover these locations in any city.

Third Spaces

In *The Great Good Place*, sociologist Ray Oldenberg, whose work explores the need for informal public gatherings in a civilized, functioning society, talks about third spaces, where people can meet and converse, and enjoy being at one with their community, in places that are neither work (second space) nor home (first space). He describes such places as where "people get together for no purpose, higher or lower, than for the 'joy, vivacity, and relief' of engaging their personalities beyond the contexts of purpose, duty, or role."

In researching her books, Siobhan observed something similar, discovering that quiet places often made it easier to talk to strangers. "Everyone I spoke to in the locations I visited shared my appreciation of quiet places—it was like belonging to a secret club where the only rules were that if you wanted to, you could share your delight about a tranquil place with someone else in the idyllic spot you'd both discovered."

Perhaps it is this desire for community that is at the heart of the need for quietness. Quiet places calm the disharmony that can be felt in work places and on daily commutes. But through them, it is also possible to experience a renewed sense of generosity and openness. In such moments, you can listen to the lull in city traffic, hear birdsong, watch with wonder how shadows fall across a courtyard, and even talk to strangers. This is the gift of a quiet place.

EXPERIENCING QUIET IN YOUR CITY

Here are some ways to escape busyness in an urban environment:

1. Enter Your Zip Code into an Online Map Search Engine
You'll discover any local gardens and parks, smaller streets and laneways that are a short walk away.

2. Share Your Quiet Places with Others
When sitting in your favorite place, speak to people nearby. Talk about your experience of quiet places in the city and invite them to share theirs.

3. Participate in Some Slow Listening
Tune into the music score of your quiet place. What do you hear? Birdsong? The muted sounds of traffic in the distance?

"Silence is the sleep that nourishes wisdom."

Francis Bacon

TEN MINUTES OF MINDFULNESS

Turn off your cell phone and sit quietly. Let thoughts emerge and pass. Simply be in the present moment. Commit to doing this several times a week.

At the end of the week, reflect on your experience. How did it feel, just to notice, without trying to change anything?

....

....

....

....

....

....

....

....

....

....

....

....

....

....

....

....

PAY ATTENTION

Take a walk and seek out beauty in the unexpected. Notice colors, textures, shadows, and reflections. Look down, look up, and look along.

What feelings and emotions do they conjure?

....

....

....

....

....

....

....

....

....

....

....

....

....

....

....

DISCOVER YOUR OWN SECRET PLACE

Locked away in every city are tranquil pockets of peace.

- Go for a walk around the place where you live or the area where you work. Take a map if you're worried about getting lost.

- Find a road you've never gone down before. Explore it. Where does it lead? What's at the end of it? Perhaps there'll be a church or a store you never knew existed. Perhaps there'll be a nature spot hidden from most people.

- If you don't find anything, keep walking until you do. Even if there's something small, the shade beneath an apple tree maybe, a view through a gap in a fence, a store selling old radios from the 1970s—it will be a place that was secret from you until now.

- Take a moment to breathe in the scene. Absorb the details. If you like, take a photograph to record it. But most of all, just be.

- Return home or back to work. Take the secret place with you throughout your day.

In the Night Garden

Sleeping outdoors as part of a vacation can heighten the senses and bring a real sense of achievement.

If you have joyful memories of childhood camping expeditions with halcyon days spent running around in the sunshine, followed by nights of solid sleep and the gentle sound of fluttering canvas, you'll know how peaceful and in tune with yourself living outdoors can make you feel. But have you ever thought of taking things a step further and sleeping outside without a tent—with no roof or shelter and nothing between you and the night sky? Proponents of outdoor sleeping suggest the experience is addictive and that the feeling of well-being induced by self-elected nighttime exposure to the elements is second to none.

Being outside is one of the ultimate sensory experiences. Allowing your eyes to linger on a long view, feeling the sting of icy wind on your cheeks, or lowering your head to listen to bubbling water, all contribute to an overall sense of well-being. The nighttime outdoor environment is no exception to this, but it also brings subtle adjustments that can both surprise and soothe the senses.

Evening air can feel fresher and smell different as cooler temperatures reduce volatile compound concentrations and night-pollinated plants release their scent. And contrary to popular belief, even in areas of low light pollution, night is rarely a place of pitch darkness, though daytime familiarities can take on a different significance when cast into shadow or limited by the distance of a flashlight's beam. As darkness takes over and the sense of sight diminishes, its companions come into play. The trickling of a nearby stream can deliver a musical lullaby, the feeling of rough tree bark under your fingers can tell an elusive story and the splash pattern of a water droplet on your face can be traced and remembered.

Sense of Freedom

Outdoor sleepers talk about experiencing a oneness with nature, that the time outside forges a connection with your surroundings, allowing you to become more in-tune with your environment's sights, smells, and sounds.

Sleeping outside, however, isn't always the easiest of options and you'd be forgiven if worry over a poor night's slumber proved too much of a deterrent. Indeed, "not sleeping much," is often cited as the main disadvantage of outdoor sleeping, particularly when the weather is less than accommodating.

When a person spends the night outside, three factors can contribute to the perception of lost sleep: they often go to bed earlier; they tend to sleep less soundly in strange locations; and if they do wake up outside, their senses can be surprised into alertness by the unfamiliar environment. Those who regularly sleep outside out of choice, however, find that the closer and more frequent acquaintance with the outdoor environment and sensory experiences increase the likelihood of longer sleeps.

Wakeful Wonder

While the amount and quality of sleep you get is important there's another wonderful element to outdoor sleeping—the quality of your wakefulness.

Finding yourself awake during a night outdoors can be wonderful. Instead of striving for sleep, learn to rest into the natural environment and look upon the wakeful moments as bonus mindfulness time. With a view restricted to the sky above you and your skin in direct contact with the elements, you can focus on your experience of the world—notice a mist stroking its way across your face, listen to pinecones dropping onto a bed of leaves, or feel hammock lines vibrating with the creakings of a tree branch. Once you've relaxed and are in tune with your senses, you'll find your body's natural response is to ease you back into slumber.

Opportunities to Learn

Outdoor sleeping can boost self-esteem as it encourages experiential learning—finding out how to keep warm, rig a hammock, or even make a hot drink outdoors with far fewer trappings—and gives a sense of achievement. It also enables the person to understand the impact, for good or bad, that fresh experiences can bring. So, it's a useful idea to try out these different things. If, for example, you find sleeping in a bivvy bag claustrophobic, try spending the night in a hammock instead. Similarly, if sleeping in a wide open space feels unnerving, think about creating a roofless shelter in the woods and see if that suits you better. You may find that, by stepping beyond your usual level of experience, you emerge feeling exalted and encouraged to extend yourself in different areas of your life as well.

TIPS FOR SAFE OUTDOOR SLEEPING

- Tell someone you trust about your plans and what time you expect to return.
- Check the weather forecast and plan accordingly.
- Don't rely on cell phones for signal, battery power, navigation, or light.
- Arrive in the daylight to help you spot potential hazards.
- Avoid sleeping by water as water levels can rise quickly.
- Take a first-aid kit.
- Dress appropriately for the conditions.
- Keep a dry set of clothes for emergencies.
- Take plenty of rations.
- Go to bed warm—eat a warm meal, layer up, enjoy a warm drink.

ESSENTIAL KIT

- Something to keep the rain out (a bivvy bag is ideal)
- Sleeping bag (suitable for the season) and mat
- Several layers of clothing, plus waterproof outerwear
- A stove to make a hot drink (with dry matches)
- High-calorie foods (to help you stay warm)
- A map and compass (if you're exploring)
- A good flashlight (head flashlights are the most useful)
- A sense of adventure

The Art of Noticing

Could something as simple as a commuter journey lead to a closer inquiry into the patterns of everyday life and a renewed personal engagement with the world?

For a moment, pause and notice the information coming in through your senses: sights, smells, sounds, the touch of clothes on your skin, the gravity of your body standing, sitting, or lying down, whether you're stationary or moving.

Notice the shift in attention as you notice. All these sensations give feedback about your body in space and time. They are anchors tying you to the present moment and adding definition to your experience. Aspects of meditation? Perhaps. But now think about recording and organizing this information in an expressive way—visually, musically, verbally, or kinesthetically. Ordinary experience becomes the essence of art.

Training Your Thoughts

Imagine you're sitting on a bus in heavy traffic. See yourself pick up a pen and start to doodle your movements as the bus lurches and creeps slowly forward. Documenting your reactions to your surroundings can shift you into a nonjudgmental stance with your experience. As you focus on a single sensation, you inadvertently form a buffer zone between your journey's beginning and its end. Regular practice could change your experience and become an inquiry into the patterns of everyday life, how they give shape and texture, and what they look like when translated into artistic elements. It might even introduce you to a way of noticing that offers a different way of traveling through your days.

Sense of Purpose

There are many ways to begin intentional noticing. Try scanning your environment, observing rhythms, looking for patterns. Choose to document color schemes, forest sounds, or sky and cloud colors. Interacting as a field observer can keep you in a healthy relationship with the world, helping you to witness the way a particular place shows up and how you connect to it.

In time, noticing patterns and routines may develop into a classic mindfulness practice. Jon Kabat-Zinn, the professor emeritus of medicine who pioneered the modern mindfulness-based approach to stress reduction, defines mindfulness as "paying attention in a particular way: on purpose, in the present moment, and nonjudgmentally." The intention of noticing draws you into the here and now as a participant in a greater flow. Introductory meditation invites the practitioner to start each session via the senses, noting sensations of touch, sound, air through the nostrils. Mindfulness training calls for cultivating a poise that is both engaged and curiously observant, as you interact with your environment. These elements can become part of your daily noticing routines.

FIND YOUR DAILY PRACTICE

Use the following exercises to develop your own noticing practices—your go-to ways of cultivating mindful engagement with your environment.

1. Pick a Routine

For a few days, select a routine to observe. Note the sequence, the predictable elements, as well as any variations and patterns. Observe any sensory experiences as you go through this routine. For instance, watch your hands as you make your coffee, smell the aroma, feel the cup, taste the coffee until it's gone. Try not to multitask, plan ahead, or ruminate about the past as you do this. Record your thoughts here.

....

....

....

....

....

....

....

....

....

....

....

....

....

....

2. Engage with Your Environment

Set aside a time each day to observe the same thing and write about it here. Choose something you can count on but that has a dynamic quality. For instance, describe the sky each morning, or the passersby in front of your home or workplace, or the birds that come to the feeder. Note your observations using descriptive words, color swatches, quick sketches, haikus, or photographs.

3. Go Through the Motions

Try your hand at motion-generated patterns. Select a drawing or painting tool and a surface, digital or analog, and a time where you are a passenger, perhaps in a train, on a bus, or in a car. As you ride, make simple marks, guided by movement. Do you notice a change in your relationship to your journey?

4. Connect Using Color

Collect a found object or photo that represents something from your environment. Create a color palette that captures the object or photo. Stop there or assign each color a number or letter. For instance, ten colors work well with numbers zero to nine, twenty-six colors would allow for twenty-six letters of the alphabet, seven colors would connect with the musical scale. Use this palette in a pattern or sequence. You can create your palette using something as straightforward as your phone number or name, or you could pick something more unfamiliar.

"Nothing can bring you peace but yourself."

Ralph Waldo Emerson

Escaping Alone

"Me time" often happens indoors—a bubble bath, a TV binge, staying tucked up in bed for the morning—but finding an hour or so to indulge yourself doesn't always have to be inside. Exploring and discovering new experiences on your own in the outside world builds confidence, makes you more independent and resilient— and boosts your well-being, too.

There is still a stigma attached to venturing out to certain places on your own— the theater, a concert, a festival—why would anyone want to be alone in a crowd? Granted, you can feel vulnerable and a little self-conscious being on your own in some situations, but in other circumstances, being alone is great for your self-confidence and your self-esteem. It gives you an ideal opportunity to simply focus on yourself.

Freedom to Act

As well as being good for the soul and allowing you time to recharge and reflect, venturing somewhere alone helps to develop your independence. A *Journal of Consumer Research* study published in 2015 encouraged people to go to an art gallery, some in groups and some alone. Before going inside the gallery, they had to predict how much they'd enjoy the experience. It turned out the people going alone enjoyed their visit far more than they'd predicted, and regardless of whether the individual was in a group or solo, everyone experienced near the same levels of enjoyment. People expect fun to come with company, but you can also enjoy exploring alone.

Nothing to See Here

Being alone can bring you refreshing anonymity, especially in busy places. It's liberating to know that you have your own plans and are only relying on yourself to make them happen. Passing by other busy people, noticing but not fully acknowledging their presence, quickly becomes easy to do. Everyone has their own place they need to get to, and essentially you're doing the same. Feeling comfortable with doing your own thing, whether enjoying a coffee in a café or embarking on a vacation abroad by yourself, will make the experience peaceful and relaxing.

Older and Wiser

Spending time on your own might mean you have to step outside of your comfort zone. Confidence in this comes with experience, which could account for the fact that older generations are often more likely to attend things alone. But why wait and let the years pass by before taking the plunge and escaping alone? If your well-being benefits from time on your own, then put the fear of what other people might think to one side and take your first steps outside. Hold your head high and get truly acquainted with yourself while doing something that you love.

FIVE THINGS YOU CAN DO BY YOURSELF

1. Attend an Arts Venue
Go to the movies or see a play, visit an exhibition or gallery—be spontaneous. Get your art fix and some inspiration for your own creative projects. The best thing about attending exhibitions alone is that you're allowed to enjoy them at your own pace, reading as much or as little information as you wish. You may also find that you get more easily lost in plays, musicals, or movies as you don't have to worry about any other person's enjoyment, simply your own. The experience becomes more personal.

2. Visit a Museum
There are a vast number of museums—established or pop-up. You are likely to find plenty of options, no matter where you live or what you can afford. Look at their websites for information about new exhibitions, or find out when visiting is free. The opportunities to seek education and expand your knowledge are endless.

3. Take a Stroll in a Green Space
Weather permitting, put on a comfortable pair of shoes and enjoy a leisurely walk alone in the peace and tranquility of the natural world. It's free, it's good exercise, and it can give your mind time to process or reflect on things you may have been putting off. You might pass people walking their dogs, families, or joggers, but one thing you can guarantee is that everyone will be absorbed in their own activities, so this may be a good choice if you're feeling anxious about the prospect of taking that first journey somewhere alone. After your walk, find a comfy spot to sit and either pull out a book or simply watch the world go by.

4. Explore Your City or Town
There's a good chance you won't be familiar with every area on your doorstep, so either turn up with an empty itinerary and see what strikes your fancy on the day, or come with a plan of places you want to see. Stop for lunch or dinner—enjoying a meal alone is possible!—or just a rest. By the time you arrive back home in the evening, you'll be glowing with happiness.

5. Go (Window) Shopping
Shopping alone allows you to browse, try on, and take your time without the pressure of considering if your company is bored and ready to move on. It might also make you look at items you normally would disregard as "not for you," and help to build your confidence. If you're in need of a friend's opinion, almost anyone can be reached in an instant by sending a photo. However, one of the great things about shopping alone is that you don't need anyone else's approval—if you feel good in the new item of clothing, then that's all you need to know to make a decision on purchasing it.

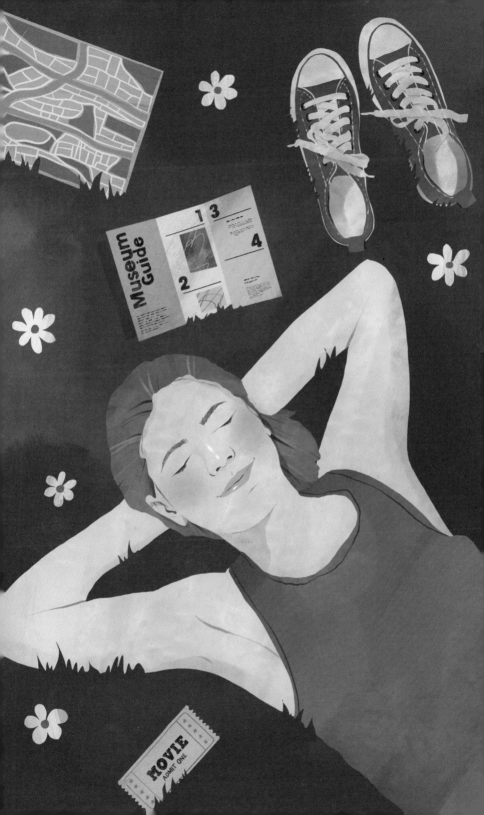

Every Breath You Take

Use mindful breathing to help feel calm and escape the chaos.

You take around 20,000 breaths a day—these are central to everything, affecting emotions and reflecting energy levels. In the West, short, shallow breathing is common, but this can lead to a higher heart rate, tense jaw and shoulders, anxiety, and digestive issues. If you notice yourself sliding into rapid "stress breaths," find time to counteract it: Sit quietly and place one hand on your chest, the other below your navel. Inhale through the nose, feeling the breath inflate the diaphragm from the bottom all the way up to your chest. Hold for a few seconds before exhaling slowly through pursed lips, while relaxing the muscles in your face, jaw, shoulders, and stomach.

BREATHE FOR PEACE AND FOCUS

Try these calming breathing exercises:

Square Breathing
This exercise can help you feel more relaxed. When you breathe in a slow, conscious way, you shift your attention from anxious thoughts and bring awareness back into your body.

- Visualize a square and follow its lines in your mind.
- Breathe in through the nose for four seconds, hold the breath for four seconds, breathe out through the nose for four seconds, hold the breath for four seconds.
- Each time imagine going along each line of the square.
- As the body calms down, you can shift from this exercise to simply being mindful of your breathing, without controlling the breath. Repeat as often and for as long as necessary.

Triangle Breathing
This exercise can be used to bring focus. In triangle breathing, the exhale (forming the triangle's base) is about twice as long as the inhale. Try counts of four-four-six to start with, building up to counts of four-four-eight.

- Imagine a triangle.
- Breathing in through the nose, imagine going up one side of the triangle, for a count of four, holding the breath for a count of four as you trace down the other side of the triangle, then exhaling slowly through the nose for a count of six or eight as you go across the bottom of the triangle.
- Repeat as often and for as long as necessary.

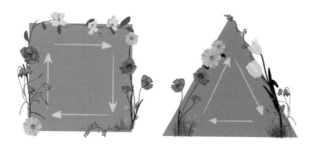

Fresh Perspectives

The multisensory movement encourages a slower, more mindful way of experiencing art

When was the last time you looked at a piece of art? Do you remember all the things you could hear, smell, taste, and feel as well as what you could see?

It's well-known that humans experience the world through their five senses. Most galleries and museums do their best to dampen four of these so that visitors can better focus on one: what they see. Their tactics are familiar. They use neutral surroundings—big, white, silent spaces—prohibit the consumption of food, and discourage touch. Despite their efforts, however, and perhaps unavoidably, those deliberately restricted senses do still come into play.

Whether it's in the smell of a grand space such as New York's Metropolitan Museum of Art, the opulent surrounds of a plush manor house like London's Wallace Collection, or the vast, echoing silence of Los Angeles' The Broad, the setting is undeniably part of the experience. Some might even say that the surrounds you associate with art galleries are comforting, they're familiar spaces that can boost positivity and a feeling of well-being.

Playing with the Senses

The multisensory art movement challenges the traditional way of consuming art, embracing all the senses rather than concentrating solely on sight, in a bid to enrich the experience and create a deeper, more resonant encounter. Of course, artists and scientists have long been fascinated with how art is experienced—installation art, which stimulates more than one sense, is far from new. But the multisensory approach challenges people to think about the way they consider pieces such as paintings and photographs, including ones that they may have seen before.

Multisensory experiences can now be found in some galleries, with visitors able to get involved in activities that will help them connect with artworks on a new level. If you like the sound of slowly taking in a piece of art, being blindfolded while trying to draw what you've just seen, and then entering into a critique of your drawing with a partner, a multisensory event might appeal. Other examples of experiences include a set menu of art-paired food and wine, and a program of music and dance inspired by a painting. It can be surprising how much more you are able to see and understand when you look slowly and across multiple senses.

Activate Body and Mind

There's been much research into the mental health benefits of creating and beholding art. As Arthur P. Shimamura, professor emeritus at the University of California, Berkeley, says, "We can appreciate art as one of those things we do simply for a pleasurable experience." And while he recognizes that human survival might not depend on art, he goes on to state that "our lives would seem so much less enjoyable without it."

The multisensory art movement aims to take this enjoyment further, but Professor Shimamura believes it's the discovery of something new that really benefits the brain. "Entirely novel experiences—such as Japanese contemporary artist Yayoi Kusama's Infinity Mirror Rooms—offer brand-new perceptual encounters, and it turns out such novel experiences activate the brain processes involved in learning and memory," he says.

Many experts point to art as a means of escape, and that when people get mindful with it they're doing good things for their health. "The slow art movement has offered a way to encourage a more thorough mental experience by forcing us to be more introspective about how an artwork impinges on our sensations, thoughts, and emotions," says Professor Shimamura.

But it's the engagement of all the senses that works the brain. He says, "The more multisensory activity in our daily lives, the more we work to integrate brain networks, and thus foster psychological well-being." If all this art exposure and sensory overloading helps you discover an artwork that resonates, it's unlikely you'll regret it. "When we get that wow feeling our whole brain and body is activated," says Professor Shimamura. "And these peak experiences enhance well-being."

A TREAT FOR ALL THE SENSES

Soak up art's endless bounty and transform any exhibition into a multisensory experience.

- Pick an artwork that you're naturally drawn to. Stand in front of it and bring all your focus to the piece. Now imagine traveling to the location or setting depicted. Visualize it clearly in your mind and picture yourself standing within it. Be there.

- Now try to imagine your wider surroundings, what can you see? Think about what might be above you and what might lie under your feet. Can you see anything beyond the frame?

- Consider the sounds or vibrations that might come to your ears inside the artwork. A landscape might have birds singing, water running, or the wind whistling. A group portrait might have chatter, laughter, or even raised voices. A sweeping, still space of modern art might hold serene or foreboding silence.

- Are you holding anything while standing in the artwork? Perhaps you've picked up an apple from a table in a still life. What does it feel like in your hands?

- Open your mouth slightly and think about the tastes that come to your lips? Have you bitten into some food or are you standing in a seascape with salt in the air?

- Go deep within the frame and consider the smells in the place depicted in the artwork. Are your nostrils being assailed by the rank odors of a polluted river, or caressed by freshly cut garden flowers in a vase?

"The principles of true art is not to portray, but to evoke."

Jerzy Kosinski

Healing Hands

Have you ever wondered why yoga teachers place their hands in certain positions or why meditators join the tips of their finger and thumb together? These symbolic hand positions are called mudras and they're an essential, fascinating part of yoga that can enhance practice and deepen understanding.

Before mats, leggings, and sparkling clean studios, there existed a tradition that looked very different to the type of yoga most popular today. This tradition didn't focus on physical feats such as handstands or backbends; instead, it turned its attention toward the workings of the mind through meditation, visualization, breathing techniques—and mudras. These gestures, made with the hands or the whole body, represent a certain intention, connect to specific elements in nature, and are most often employed within meditation practices to enhance focus. When used alone throughout the day, mudras serve as a valuable way to concentrate the mind and create an energetic shift. They can be simple, like the palms-together prayer position found throughout most cultures, or more complex symbols involving the whole body. Traditional yogic texts expound several types of mudras, ranging from those using the hands and head to ones that include bandhas or body locks that direct the flow of energy.

EVERY MUDRA HOLDS A STORY

Observe an image of any religious deity and you'll see they're often depicted holding a specific mudra. Although widely regarded as originating in India, almost all cultures use these hand gestures alongside meditation and ritual.

Abhaya Mudra

In the Buddhist tradition, they're used as a way to deepen meditation practices and as a symbol of blessing and protection. One of the most well-known mudras is featured on figures of the Buddha himself, in the form of abhaya mudra—representing fearlessness and protection.

The Hamsa Hand

Found throughout the Middle East and North Africa, this is often used in jewelry and wall hangings, depicting an open right hand. With the fingers pointing downward, the image represents protection, while an open palm with fingers pointing upward is said to indicate the giving of blessings and good luck.

Adoration Mudra

Ancient Egyptian hieroglyphs and paintings include the adoration mudra, used in their version of the Sun Salutation—similar to the yogic Surya Namaskar from India. A gesture of greeting, hands are held in front of, or slightly above or below, the face, fingers are upward, and palms face outward.

Prana Mudra and Prithvi Mudra

Appearing in Orthodox iconography, these hand gestures are seen as particularly healing, with prana enhancing the flow of life force and encouraging a healthy immune system and prithvi used for strengthening and healing, as well as enlivening the root chakra, which enables the practitioner to feel more stable and grounded.

HOW TO PUT IT INTO PRACTICE

Some mudras are used throughout a physical yoga practice, others are adopted during rituals and many more are harnessed during meditation to focus the mind. They can also be employed in everyday life to bring about mindfulness and cultivate a more positive mindset. Try following the three described here while focusing on what they represent—sit quietly in meditation or use them throughout the day when you need to shift your state of mind.

1. Prana

Prana means "life force" and refers to the essence of vitality that runs through all living things. Well-functioning prana enables each person to feel well, vibrant, and healthy. It also refers to the breath and this mudra may serve as a useful reminder to breathe fully. To practice, bring the tip of the thumb and tips of the ring and little fingers to touch. Focus on breathing slowly in and out through the nose, visualizing life-force energy flowing through your body.

2. Ganesh

Referring to the elephant-headed Hindu deity, known as the remover of obstacles, this mudra is called upon to help metaphorically clear the path ahead so that any upcoming event or journey will run smoothly. It can be used just before any challenging situation or perhaps if you're embarking upon a new direction in life. To practice, clasp each hand's fingers together at the chest, one hand facing your body and one hand facing away, with the elbows pointed out to the sides. Visualize your path ahead being free of obstacles and repeat this affirmation: "The path ahead is clear."

3. Bhu

This mudra links to the earth element and has a strong sense of being grounded and calm. With a digital world and many people spending time in their heads, bhu can serve as a way to become embodied and settled again. If possible, practice this outside to reconnect to the physical earth. Sit on the ground and bring the hands into loose fists with the middle and index fingers pointing downward. Connect the fingers to the ground and focus on allowing your body to relax into the earth. Breathe slowly and deeply, visualizing your body rooting deep into the ground.

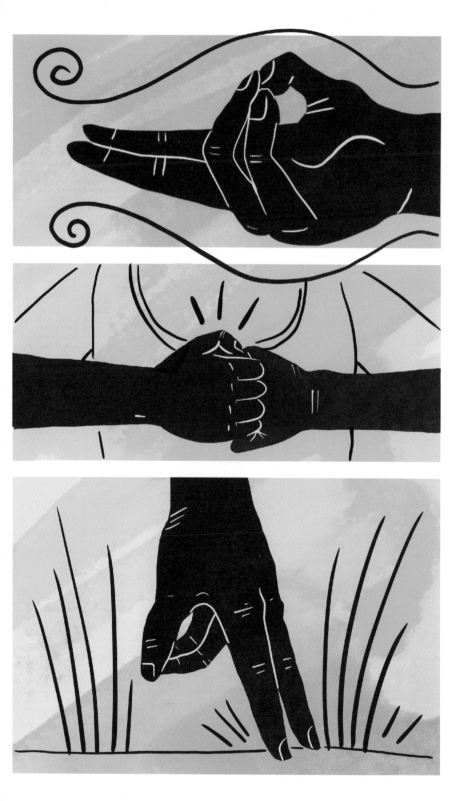

"Have nothing in your house that you do not know to be useful or believe to be beautiful."

William Morris

Make a House a Home

Making small aesthetic changes to a living space in line with the seasons can breathe fresh life into any home. Most importantly, it can bring about an improvement in both well-being and state of mind.

Experts agree that having a house that feels like a home is good for health and well-being. "Making a home a personal sanctuary is about creating a space where one can rest, relax, and connect to their essence," explains Grace Winteringham, the cofounder of Patternity, a London-based conscious-creative organization that inspires positive living through pattern research and design. "When surrounded with things that bring you joy and you love—be it patterns, colors, objects, fragrance, and sound—your senses are nourished and your overall well-being is improved."

And yet the importance of the home environment is often overlooked. "Our exterior space directly impacts well-being, and design choices affect quality of comfort on three levels: cognitive, physical, and emotional," shares Elena Grigoriou, an interior designer and sustainability and well-being expert. "For example, logical thinking and detail-oriented processes require lower ceilings, enclosed spaces, and sharp edges, while creativity and inspiration needs higher ceilings and curved shapes."

Just as our circadian rhythms affect sleep patterns and energy levels, the cyclical nature of the seasons influences well-being. Making tweaks to the home can help ease the process of adaptation throughout the year.

Dark Materials

When it comes to the practical steps that can be taken in the home, there are plenty of options. Elena highlights the Mediterranean approach of using tiled flooring with rugs that can be moved in and out of spaces depending on the weather. "Tiled floors keep the home cool in the summer while thick rugs feel warm underfoot in winter," she explains. Grace agrees, and suggests switching fabric choices across soft furnishings as the seasons change. "Heavier knits and darker tones are more suited for winter and lighter linens and looser patterns work better for spring and summer," she advises.

Power of Color

Changing color within the home environment can play a huge role. "Each color conveys its own unique message and meaning, influencing us both psychologically and physiologically," says Leatrice Eiseman, executive director of the Pantone Color Institute, the leading international authority on color. "Our research has found 95 percent of the time the influence of color takes place outside conscious awareness, meaning we don't even realize how, when, and why we respond the way we do to this universal, yet silent language."

Leatrice explains how specific colors, especially those in the yellow family, can shift your frame of mind. "Yellows can add brightness and happiness. Painting one wall (or a room if you're feeling adventurous) in a warm color will improve mood and open up a dark or cramped space," she says.

A Home for All Seasons

Grace also recommends decluttering as the seasons change—spring, it seems, is indeed the time for cleaning. "A spring clean could include changing out cushions and colors, packing away the winter wardrobe and using lighter colors in the space," Grace suggests.

"Lightness and a cleansed feeling also come through the physical clearing and letting go of things that we may no longer need. Reducing, recycling, repairing, or donating unwanted things will awaken a more conscious approach," she adds.

Investing time in a home refresh may seem like hard work at first, but the benefits to well-being are plentiful.

SPRING INTO ACTION

Follow these sustainable and affordable tips for making a home feel
ready for lighter days.

Refresh Bedding
Choose quilts and blankets that are bright and light to help the bedroom feel
more spring-like. White, creams, yellows, or bold patterns all work well.

Utilize Hanging Textiles
A hanging rail allows for season-appropriate wall art. Switch fabrics throughout
the year or hang up a winter quilt that might be too heavy to have on the bed
during the summer.

Adjust Home Fragrances

Scented candles, incense, or diffusers are an easy way to set a mood. The winter months in particular call for warming scents like vanilla, cinnamon, and amber, while spring and summer cry out for uplifting florals and citrus fruits.

Relocate Plants and Embrace the Outdoors

Moving houseplants to different rooms can change a space entirely. Think about the added light and warmth of spring when relocating plants. Make the most of flowers and display bunches in colorful vases as a reminder of the excitement and the new beginnings on the way.

Declutter

Organize linen, sort out wardrobes and drawers, file away paperwork, tidy drawers of odds and ends, and clear out kitchen and bathroom cupboards. Streamlining for the new season is good for body and mind.

Reorganize Bookshelves

Color-coordinate books based on the season and feel inspired to read titles that may have been forgotten.

Swap Cushion Covers, Drapes, Light Shades, or Rugs

Much like having summer and winter bedding, think about having cold and warm versions of soft furnishing items. Velvet, wool, and thicker weaves are lovely and cozy in winter; linens and cottons work better in the warmer months. Pop into your local vintage or thrift stores to keep purchases sustainable, and think about colors and designs.

Repaint the Front Door

Choose a spring-worthy hue to offer an instantaneous welcome and set a positive mood for anyone that enters.

Upcycle Furniture

Paint a piece of tired-looking furniture in a happy color. It will give it a new lease of life.

Rearrange a Room

Moving a couch or armchair can change the feeling of an entire room. In spring, think about positioning furniture to face the outdoors to make the most of longer and sunnier days.

Have a Summer Bedroom

For those lucky enough to have two bedrooms, switching between them each summer and winter can be a nice idea. Make one room light, airy, and bright for summer and the other warm and cozy for winter.

How Do You Doodle?

There may be more to all that seemingly random scribbling than meets the eye.

You're in a meeting, someone has been talking for half an hour about a subject that isn't relevant to you, and, whoops—you've just covered your whole notebook page in scribbles. Or perhaps you didn't, even though you wanted to, because isn't that what schoolchildren do? Wrong. Doodling is good for you, even if you're an adult.

What's in a Scribble?

Doodling is what we do when we're not really thinking about what we're doing. According to graphologist Tracey Trussell, it can be categorized as "unrefined drawings or scribbles which we create subliminally." The urge to doodle often results from being bored and Tracey believes it's "a type of proactive daydreaming—a way for the brain to find an outlet."

It's thought the desire to doodle is innate. Experts believe that humans used drawings before developing language, so perhaps scribbling is hardwired into the brain. Despite all the technology available to our fidgety fingertips, even now we still feel the need to doodle. There's something tangible about putting pen to paper and, whether you're an artist or not, doodling is a form of expression on a different level to anything else.

True Colors

Doodling is also pressure-free. It takes us back to that liberated state enjoyed as children, at a time in life when it's easier to try things out without wondering where they're going or worrying about wasting time on something fruitless. This is all part of the magic, according to Tracey. "Unlike handwriting," she says, "doodles are not composed for any particular recipient, which means they are unselfconscious, uncontrived, and candid. However basic or mundane a doodle may appear, it has 100 percent integrity."

Perhaps that's why so many great ideas have been formed on the back of a napkin or on a sticky note. Many people are familiar with the pressure of the blank page, but when you're producing a seemingly throwaway creation and not worried about the final result, you're able to generate a pure form of expression. "Doodling is also like a silent brainstorm device, helping us to drum up light-bulb moments and stimulate mental function for improved memory and mental clarity," Tracey says.

This is likely why doodles are so valuable when it comes to the way they affect the brain and what can be deciphered from them. Working as someone who is able to comprehend these scribbles, Tracey reveals that "if you can interpret the meaning of the shapes on the page, the insights are surprisingly far-reaching."

What Are the Benefits?

Doodling has the ability to take you from frantic head fuzz to a state of pure focus. It has the potential to bring a person into the present, all with only a pen and a piece of paper. "Studies show that doodling is therapeutic," says Tracey. She adds that it aids relaxation, gives you a moment to be mindful, and it can help you to release tension and stress. Tracey also often sees how doodling can act as a "channel for expressing repressed emotions" or as a safety net for "releasing negative feelings, allowing the brain to reset."

Doodles can also help you to work through worries and anxieties. One of their greatest values is their ability to provide an outlet during times when you can't find the words to aid or express what you might be going through. You're probably familiar with seeing artists pouring their hearts and souls onto the canvas, but did you know that the mere mortals among us can do it, too? If you're dealing with trauma or having a difficult time, doodling can offer a release.

Freudian Scrawls

Doodling might even be a hard line into your psyche. Tracey calls doodling the "language of the right brain." She compares doodles to Freudian slips, because of their telltale glimpses into the subconscious. Even if you've drawn something you think looks mundane and everyday, it still signals what you're thinking and feeling, showcasing fears or concerns you might have and sometimes revealing your deepest secrets.

"You could say that doodles are like little maps that guide us in the exploration of people's psyches," she says. "If you can translate and interpret the symbols on the page, you're getting inside someone's head."

"It gives me such a sense of peace to draw; more than prayer, walks, anything."

Sylvia Plath

DOODLE IT YOURSELF

Traditionally seen as something we do subconsciously, deciding to doodle is different from doing it organically. However, this method is often used to reset the brain and rewire attitudes and emotions, so it can still help to improve well-being. Here are a few things you might try:

- Repetitive doodling can aid relaxation, so begin by drawing lines or basic shapes, such as circles, squares, triangles, or combinations of them all. Don't worry about the complexity— this is just a starting point.

- Take note of how the shapes make you feel. Try not to judge their appearance, go with your instinct, and keep in mind Tracey's advice: "A true doodle is drawn continuously, without lifting the pen from the page."

- Once you have some shapes, try shading them. Take note afterward of the kind of pressure you've used, whether it's light or heavy and how that makes you feel. Tracy notes that shading is seen psychologically as tension release, stating that "the firmer the pen strokes, the deeper the anxiety."

- Try letting the shapes evolve into something more. They might turn into recognizable objects such as flowers, clouds, or faces, but they could also be abstract.

Turn the page to start doodling.

SCRIBBLE SPACE

Grab a pen or pencil and draw your doodles here.

When you've spent enough time doodling, come away from your creation and look at what you have scribbled. Think about what emotions it provokes.

If you'd like to try more traditional doodling, keep a pen handy for moments when you're bored or daydreaming. You might be on the phone or waiting for someone—or you could be trying to work through something difficult. Let your thoughts guide your pen and see where it takes you.

Weekend Wonders

Imagine a free weekend with no plans, no responsibilities, and no errands to run. Sound heavenly? What if it happened this weekend, though—what would you do with that glorious expanse of open, immediate future to fill as you please?

It may be tempting to lie on the couch, watch movies, and loll about. But you could live in the moment and seize those two days, filling them with activities that are good for your soul. Take the time to have fun, pamper yourself, or try something new. Great things can happen on those spontaneous days when you decide to embrace the hours ahead with no expectations or worries, so try to make it a weekend that will enhance your well-being.

TAKING TIME OUT

Stuck for inspiration? Here are a few ideas:

1. Walk This Way

Getting out into the fresh air and exploring nature is a wonderful way to exercise while giving yourself dedicated thinking time. One of the best things about rambling is that little planning and equipment is required—just pop on a good pair of walking shoes or sneakers, pack a backpack of essentials, and you're ready to go, either alone, with a dog, or any willing friends. You could head somewhere you already know, search online for an interesting local walk, or discover more about a place you've always wanted to visit.

As you stroll, turn on your senses. Focus on the light in the sky, the shape of the clouds, or tree tops moving in the breeze. What do you see, smell, and feel?

....

....

....

....

....

....

....

....

....

....

....

....

2. Cook Up a New Dish

Weekends are the perfect time to experiment with new recipes or to try some home baking. Either cook for yourself or, if you're feeling confident (and generous), invite friends or family round to sample your concoctions. While you cook, pause to smell each of the ingredients, breathing in their fragrance. Making food needn't always be rushed. Be mindful as you stir a sauce, knead some dough, or slice a vegetable. Use each step in the recipe to anchor yourself to the here and now. When you remove the dish from the oven, employ your senses to decide if it's ready.

- Is it browned to your liking?
- Does it smell delicious?
- Can you hear the bubbling inside?

As you breathe in the smell of the dish, notice where your thoughts lead you. Does the aroma remind you of meals you've had before? Or are you starting to imagine how it will taste? Reflect on your experience here.

....

....

....

....

....

Think about all the foods and flavors you haven't yet tasted. What world cuisines would you most like to try?

➤ ....

....

➤ ....

....

➤ ....

....

3. Pamper Yourself

Relax and unwind. Perhaps enjoy a bubble bath surrounded by candles with quiet music playing in the background; maybe visit a spa and experience a soothing massage. A free weekend can be used to indulge yourself, whether that's a beauty treatment at home or a trip to a salon. Impromptu treats can give you a real boost, making you feel radiant, inside and out.

What's your idea of pampering?

....

....

....

....

....

....

....

List the activities that help you relax.

▶ ....

....

▶ ....

....

▶ ....

....

▶ ....

....

4. Pretend To Be a Tourist

Spending a weekend acting like a tourist in your own backyard can be fun and open your eyes to things you miss every day. Don't overthink it, just walk to your nearest bus stop and step on the first one that arrives. Try and find a seat by the window and focus on the journey. You might be surprised by things you observe on your way that you've never noticed before. Stay on for ten stops and see where you end up.

Some routine is good, but ingrained habits can sometimes hold you back from trying new things. Do you take the same route to work every day? Or do you always eat the same things for lunch? Think about your daily patterns of behavior and list them here.

....

....

....

....

....

....

What changes could you make to your routine?

....

....

....

....

....

....

....

5. Unwind Your Mind

For the ultimate way to de-stress, unplug any electronic devices. It's easy to become consumed by the noise of other people's lives and opinions, and switching off will give you a chance to focus on yourself again.

No scrolling in the first hour of the day, no social media after 9:00 p.m.—how did it feel to spend less time on your devices? What other rules could you set to help you cut back on screen time?

....

....

....

....

....

....

....

....

....

....

....

....

....

....

....

....

6. Try a Yoga Exercise

At the end of a stressful week, practice activities that nurture your mind and emotional health. Meditation, yoga, and mindfulness will feel soothing and calming, and give you a sense of inner peace.

- Sit on the floor, legs stretched out straight in front of you with your heels pushing forward and toes skyward. With your hands gently resting on the floor beside your hips, take a few deep breaths and observe how your body feels.

- On an inhale, lift your arms above your head, raising your upper torso skyward.

- On an exhale, fold forward from your hips, keeping your spine straight as you move toward your feet. Gently rest your upper torso on the top of your legs with your head touching down last. Wrap your arms around your feet or ankles. (At first, it may be difficult to fully release over your legs; therefore just release and reach forward to a point that is comfortable. With practice, you'll find that your extension forward will increase, and you will be able to stretch further.)

- Come out of the pose on an inhale. From your hips slowly raise your torso back up to a seated position, vertebrae by vertebrae, with your head coming up last and your arms flowing back up and round to rest alongside your body.

- Take a few deep breaths here and observe how your body feels. Notice if you're experiencing less tension and feel more relaxed in your being.

"Smile, breathe, and go slowly."

Thích Nhất Hanh

7. Get Creative

Use the opportunity to tap into your creative side, whether that's painting with watercolors, jewelry making, photography, or knitting. Did you enjoy creative subjects at school? Is there a craft you've always wanted to try, or do you have a yearning to be a writer or a poet? Focusing on a creative project has the potential to bring feelings of accomplishment regardless of the end result.

Do you have a tale to tell? Why not write a short story? Map out key points, events, and characters here. How will you keep readers intrigued until the happy or sad ending?

....

....

....

....

....

....

....

....

....

....

....

....

....

....

PLAN AHEAD

Use this space to jot down ideas of what you'd like to do next time you find yourself with an unexpected free weekend.

....

....

....

....

....

....

....

....

....

....

....

....

"Keep good company, read good books, love good things, and cultivate soul and body as faithfully as you can."

Louisa May Alcott

"Though we travel the world over to find the beautiful, we must carry it with us, or we find it not."

Ralph Waldo Emerson

Sky's the Limit

If you tend to keep your gaze downward or fixed firmly ahead, it's possible you're missing out on one of nature's most awe-inspiring and natural remedies.

Whatever the weather, whatever the time, step outside right now and look up. Because wherever you are, you'll see one of the planet's most extraordinary sights—the sky. We absorb the view into our lives, grumbling if it ushers in too many rain clouds, sweltering when it fails to deliver enough protection from a harsh sun. It's an incredible, vast, ever-changing, and majestic source of wonder. Yet this vision of extraordinary in the ordinary is more often than not missed. It takes a conscious effort to notice the sky, which is a shame, as the feelings of awe it can evoke are said to contribute to well-being.

The Oxford English Dictionary describes awe as "a feeling of reverential respect mixed with fear or wonder," with philosophers and religious scholars having long noted its ability to boost mind, body, and soul. It wasn't until 2003, however, that psychologists Dacher Keltner and Jonathan Haidt presented a formalized version of this concept. Since then, researchers at the University of California (UC), Berkeley's Greater Good Science Center have been exploring and documenting its effects. And studies have revealed that feeling a sense of awe can reduce anxiety and stress, while boosting traits such as generosity through an increased sense of oneness. And in doing so, overall physical health is also improved, thanks to a drop in stress hormones.

Heavens Above

Most people, however, find the idea of going out and seeking awe to be a challenging prospect. It's easy to miss the awe-inspiring in everyday life and feel as though it's necessary to go somewhere special and do something amazing to reap its benefits. Researcher and psychotherapist Paul Conway is hoping to prove otherwise—that all we have to do is stay put and look upward. He has developed an innovative area of awe-based research, named skychology, that's committed solely to the sky and its role in the enhancement of well-being. By understanding what people experience when they look up at this seemingly infinite natural resource, he hopes to create accessible, everyday interventions designed to boost happiness.

"Because awe is based on the mystery of existence, experiencing it—even infrequently—is an elusive endeavor for many," says Paul. "So, I asked myself how we could all experience this feeling more often in our daily lives. I believe an answer may be on the horizon in the form of skychology. My studies suggest that this is an always-open window into the experience of awe and, therefore, enhanced well-being. As we simultaneously witness the infinite and impermanent of the sky above, we are able to experience all the benefits of awe that might otherwise feel hard to come by."

A Simple Science

Whereas other wellness practices might seem time-consuming to work into a busy schedule, skychology offers the potential for a ready dose of daily well-being. You can enjoy it on the way to work, taking the dog for a walk, or running weekly errands. There's no equipment required, no need to even find five minutes of peace—although a moment of quietude can help when learning how to shift into an awe-receptive headspace. All you have to do is look up, observe, and appreciate. The studies performed by both Paul and UC Berkeley's research team suggest that doing so can bring an instant and cumulative boost to physical and emotional health.

In California, researchers tested the impact awe has on cytokines—proteins that interact with the immune system and regulate inflammatory responses. They discovered that awe-inspiring experiences reduced levels of inflammatory responses in subjects to a statistically significant degree. They also appeared to induce the release of the hormone oxytocin, which helps to relieve anxiety and depression, decrease pain, and improve digestion.

Experiencing awe via skychology also offers a feeling of connectedness, which can bring a positive emotional lift that appears to grow with repeated sky-gazing. "The process of self-diminishment which occurs in the face of awe found through skychology makes us feel smaller and humbler, cultivating a greater sense of perspective and humility," explains Paul. "Simply gazing at the sky and appreciating it for all that it is promotes prosocial behaviors through a greater sense of connection to others, to nature, and the world around us—all of which are integral dimensions of psychological well-being."

See Things Differently

Shifting your perspective into an awareness where you truly understand how incredible, mysterious, and, at times, terrifying the sky can be, is all it takes to start enjoying the benefits. To make it easier, start with a vibrant or striking sky—perhaps at sunrise or sunset, when the sun's rays pour through hazy clouds in a heavenly display, mid-torrential rainstorm, or a snowy blizzard. You could choose a clear, starry night or an evening when a breathtaking supermoon is set to brighten the way. Take a moment to clear your mind of thoughts, look up, and just be with the sky. Think about how tiny we are in comparison to its majesty, how little we know about it, and how we have no control over its powerful nature. Take in the colors and textures, the movement, sounds, and sensations of the surrounding weather. Over time, with daily practice, observing the world above you will feel easier regardless of your emotional state and how good, bad, or ordinary your day has been. An instantly accessible state of awe can become a fixture in daily life.

Experience the Extraordinary in the Ordinary

At first, you'll need to commit a few minutes to go outside and gaze up at the sky, uninterrupted. A little privacy can also make things easier. Soon, however, it will be possible to glance upward anywhere at any time and get straight in the zone.

START PRACTICING

This activity works any time—day or night—whatever your mood and with or without company.

- Take a couple of deep breaths, breathing in through the nose and out through the mouth, and look up.

- Be curious and notice what you see. Let thoughts and feelings come and go as you notice the sky. No effort is required.

- Enjoy doing this for as little or as long as you like. The sky is constantly changing, just like our emotions. Every experience will be unique.

- Notice how you feel afterward and the way in which it differs from your feelings beforehand.

LOOK THROUGH A LENS OF CURIOSITY

Approaching skychology with an attitude of inquisitiveness can be helpful when seeking awe. Noticing all the unique and ever-changing details of the sky, pondering how and why it constantly transforms, and the impact that it has on individuals and the world as a whole, will deepen the experience. Here are some ideas to help elevate curiosity, the resulting awe and its benefits.

- Observe the varying colors, shapes, shadows, and areas of contrasts or sameness you can see. How quickly or slowly are any clouds moving?

- What changes can you notice since the last time you looked at the sky? Does it have a tendency to reflect how you're feeling? Or is it different?

- What appears at first glance to be a drab, overcast sky can be fascinating when viewed through the lens of curiosity. Think about the positive impact the current sky (however it looks) might be having on the world.

Use this space to record your thoughts.

Seeds of Change

Habits and preferences can take root and become immovable, making change feel impossible. But any small step into the unknown encourages fresh growth and can help you to break free.

Trees have enthralled and inspired people around the world for millennia. Even today, countless societies and cultures imbue these tall and often ancient giants with wisdom. But what has prompted so many poets, novelists, artists, and moviemakers to personify them through the years? Which of their qualities suggest an aura of intellect? Perhaps the stillness of trees is an indicator of how they have watched over the landscape for centuries. Upon extending their roots deep into the soil beneath, trees remain planted—both literally and figuratively—in one place for their entire life.

Remaining in one spot for extended periods is not something people share with their woody counterparts—humans have always roamed, moving town, country, or even continent. Some relish and embrace the lack of constraint and opportunity for transformation, others find it difficult. For them, stepping into the unknown is a sensitive endeavor, requiring a deep breath and much bravery. Yet change remains an important part of life and is worthy of celebration.

Gathering Moss

In Lucy Maud Montgomery's classic *Anne of Green Gables* series, the eponymous lead loves being surrounded by nature, particularly trees. Set in the Canadian province of Prince Edward Island, the sweeping scenery keeps her young, wandering mind content. Yet even this orphaned teenager comes to see that change is inevitable. As her neighbor Mr. Harrison says in *Anne of Avonlea*, "Changes ain't totally pleasant but they're excellent things. Two years is about long enough for things to stay the same. If they stayed put any longer, they might grow mossy." If we were to take Mr. Harrison's musings to heart, it invites this question: what needs to be done to avoid "growing moss" in daily life?

First, it's important not to mistake moss with fungi which, in the context of trees, can provide nutrients and help with growth. Similarly for humans, if something akin to healthy fungi supports well-being, then it's probably worth maintaining. Knowing what really needs to be altered and whether it's currently beneficial to you or not is paramount, as change for the sake of it can be counterproductive. In other words, "If it ain't broke, don't fix it."

Yet when the same old, same old begins to take its toll and no longer feels fulfilling, the moment might come when the moss has to be cleared. There is no one way of going about such a task. Nor, for that matter, will the results be the same for everyone—we all lead different lives. You get to define how significant the change is, with none too big or small to fit your personal definition. It could be scaling back work projects to make more time for family and friends, swapping cardio classes for Pilates, or spending more time with your nose in a book than looking at the TV—it could even just be rearranging photos on a shelf. The only important thing is that it's significant to you.

Act SMART

It can be useful to use the acronym SMART when considering your goals.
Ask yourself if what you're altering is specific, measurable, achievable,
realistic, and time-bound.

- Specific rather than broad changes will enable you to make positive steps—large or small.
- Measurable rather than boundless objectives will keep you motivated.
- Achievable aims are less likely to discourage you.
- Realistic goals are easier to maintain.
- Time-bound goals shouldn't stretch into infinity—give them a deadline.

Avonlea resident Mr. Harrison alludes to the idea of making a significant change
at least once every two years. While an admirable aspiration, this might not work
for everyone. Be patient and kind to yourself when things take longer. Likewise,
if goals fall into place quicker than initially imagined, enjoy the moment. And
take comfort in knowing that you and that mighty oak in the forest, or perhaps
the resilient willow by the riverside, are both worthy and deserving of growth.

CLEAR THE MOSS

If you're on the cusp of a purposeful change, or wish to work toward one, ask yourself the following questions and jot down your thoughts.

Could this change be beneficial and/or fulfilling?

....

....

....

....

....

....

Does it meet my personal definition of significant?

....

....

....

....

....

....

....

....

....

....

Is it SMART?

....

....

....

....

....

....

When change is slow—am I being patient and kind to myself?

....

....

....

....

....

When change is quick, am I appreciating each moment along the way?

....

....

....

....

....

....

....

Mind the Trap

There can be a tendency to fill the gaps of memory with your own narrative, but this can lead you into a maze of biased beliefs from which it's difficult to escape.

What are the first words that come to mind when trying to describe someone who's telling lies? Insincere, unfair, dishonest? Although lies and honesty are normally thought of as being at odds with each other, and saying the opposite is likely to raise some eyebrows, confabulation is a term that comprises the two—it's what the mind does when trying to make sense of the events in the surrounding world, which results in an "honest lie." If this wasn't enough of a surprise, it also seems that these "lies" appear in communication between people more often than expected.

What's a Confabulation?

To fully understand the term, it's important to begin by noting the weight it carries in a medical setting. First used as a technical term by German neurologists Karl Bonhoeffer, Arnold Pick, and Carl Wernicke in the early 1900s, confabulation is used in the context of memory disorders. In medical terms, it's a symptom when a person fills in any gaps in memory with false information, in psychology, it's seen as an error in recollection, as a result of which fabricated events are created. This is different from lying, as a person who confabulates is unaware of the information being false and sincerely believes it to be true.

For example, do you remember a time when a colleague failed to respond to your morning greeting and you were quick to assume it was because they didn't like you? Or an occasion when you were interrupted during a meeting and you told yourself it was because your ideas weren't good enough? Both of these are examples of confabulations.

You honestly believed these explanations to be true when you were telling them to yourself or others—however, they were most likely lies. The colleague was daydreaming about that first cup of morning coffee and your contribution during the meeting sparked a brilliant follow-up idea.

Confabulations outside of its medical meaning can often be influenced by a psychological bias called a confirmation trap. In simple terms, this is one of the games that the mind plays when it looks for evidence to confirm existing beliefs instead of seeking reasons why they might be wrong. This bias is so strong that it can make you focus only on the evidence that reinforces these existing views, blocking out anything that denies them, without you realizing that something is being overlooked. Research shows that even when the counterevidence is pointed out, a confirmation trap makes it hard to change your opinion.

Why Is This Important?

These honest lies that you might be telling yourself and the confirmation trap that the mind has prepared for you are likely to be reinforcing those false, often self-limiting beliefs that can affect your work, relationships, and overall well-being. Just pause for a moment to think about how many misunderstandings or conflicts you would have avoided by not engaging in a likely false narrative of the mind. How many opportunities might you have taken if it wasn't for that self-defeating belief you thought you saw confirmed repeatedly?

Searching for the Truth

By being aware of what the brain is capable of, you can start challenging these mind games when they happen, instead of believing a false reality. Confirmation bias is a trap with no hope to escape from unless you are aware of its existence and pay attention to it, as only then can you start looking for ways to overcome it. It's comforting to believe that the surrounding world can always be fully understood and correctly interpreted at all times by looking at it through your own lens. It feels good to be right and know it all, as that's exactly what the mind loves the most—clarity and a full story for any situation.

However, these stories and any gaps in between are likely to be filled in with confabulations—honest lies that you might be telling yourself and others, that either lack evidence or are based on subjective evidence created by a mind that's trapped in a confirmation bias. Luckily, you can choose to escape these mind traps by being mindful and following a few of the tips outlined on the right.

HOW CAN YOU ESCAPE THE TRAP?

Awareness is the first step toward more objective thinking, which is free from the honest lies and the confirmation trap, which the mind finds so comforting. From here, you can take one step further and practice self-reflection by trying to do the following:

1. Pause

Take a moment to think about the stories you tend to tell yourself. Can you recognize any patterns? Is there anything those stories have in common? Be aware that any reoccurring themes are likely to be honest lies you tell yourself consistently, that only serve to reinforce any existing self-limiting beliefs.

2. Think Factually

Every time you notice your mind engaging in a narrative trying to explain behaviors or reactions of those around you, try to focus on the facts. Ask yourself questions such as:

- What do I know for sure?
- What am I making up?
- Why am I making this story up even though there is no factual evidence supporting this version of events?

3. Practice Not Knowing

If there's no factual information to support a story you're telling yourself, don't be afraid to admit there's something you're not certain about or can't explain. Similarly to thinking factually and asking yourself to reflect on things you know for sure, take the opposite angle and use words such as:

- I am not sure about this.
- What I don't know for sure is . . .

4. Ask Questions

If you have any concerns about something that's said or the way someone behaves around you, voice your questions instead of jumping to conclusions that are likely to be a result of a trapped mind. These questions won't come across as confrontational if you focus on a situation and question based on the facts rather than your assumptions or emotions. Opening these questions with the following phrases can be particularly useful:

- Am I right to believe this?
- Do I understand this correctly?
- Am I correct to think that?

5. Be Curious

Acknowledging that your way of perceiving the world around you is just one of the 7.8 billion ways to perceive it will enable you to keep an open mind and discover new ways of looking at things. Learning to be open to new perspectives will challenge a confirmation bias and empower you with an open mind rather than a trapped one.

Be Transported

Immersive literature allows you to explore far and wide without stepping outside your front door.

As anyone who has lost the early hours of a morning to a good book knows, it's easy to become entirely absorbed by a captivating novel. While it's often a deft opening line, an intriguing character, or a mystery to be unpicked that initially hooks the reader, it's the all-embracing description of place that reels them in and takes them to a world far removed from their current reality. Using the five senses, books introduce us to new towns, new countries, new people. It's an unparalleled experience, a way to explore the world without ever having to leave our front door.

Books also provide a respite from the everyday even when their characters are challenging or their stories are based on real-life events. Bibliotherapist and book curator Bijal Shah, who prescribes literature as a form of therapy, highlights the common experience that reading provides—a vehicle for truly losing yourself. "In a book you become a passerby who is able to watch a story without being connected to it," she says. "You feel free when reading a book. It's liberating to make judgments without consequence. You can empathize with a character without being wary of that person."

Making a Connection

The concentration and focus that reading requires also makes it a stress-busting exercise, whether you're sitting in your living-room armchair or lying on a sunlounger. This is because reading is so much more than a single activity. While every action in the brain is localized, reading uses a number of those individual actions—visual, auditory, fluency, and comprehension—simultaneously.

On top of this, separate research suggests that reading about certain situations or experiences activates the brain in the same way as if we were actually doing them. A study at Carnegie Mellon University, Pennsylvania, scanned the brains of eight people as they read a chapter in *Harry Potter and the Sorcerer's Stone* where the young wizard has his first flying lesson. The researchers discovered that the sequence activated the part of the brain connected with motion. While it's still unclear as to how this connection is created, it goes some way to explaining why books can be so compelling—they enable readers to experience real-life situations via imaginative writing, transporting them to a different time, a different place.

Take, for example, Barbara Kingsolver's *Lacuna*, a fictional tale of a young American boy called Harrison Shepherd who ends up working in the home of the artists Frida Kahlo and Diego Rivera in Mexico City in the 1930s. From the azure blue walls of their shared home and the shaded streets of suburban Coyoacán, to the bustling markets and sizzling street vendors, the author delivers you to the Mexican capital.

GO SLOW

By taking your time and traveling back over paragraphs once, twice, three times, a book's true magic can be released.

- Discovering which books are best for slow reading is an act of reflection and self-awareness, and can be a delight in itself.

- Set aside at least half an hour a week for slow reading. Choose a time and place where you won't be interrupted.

- Turn your phone down and put it in a bag or a drawer. It may take a few minutes to settle, but persist.

- If you find yourself racing ahead, return to the previous page and read it again, more slowly.

Perfect Scents

The best descriptive prose often uses the five senses to evoke a particular place. Scent, the oldest and more powerful of the five, arguably has the greatest power to transport the reader. Just think of the whiff of a favorite childhood recipe or the aroma of a teenage perfume and the emotions it conjures up. Experiencing scent through writing can have an equally potent effect. In fact, one study from Jaume I University in Valencia, Spain, found that when participants read odor-related words like garlic, cinnamon, or jasmine, the primary olfactory cortex (the area of the brain that processes smell) lit up.

In her semiautobiographical novel *The God of Small Things*, Arundhati Roy takes her reader to the southern Indian state of Kerala with scent-led descriptions of local flowers, monsoons, and the central family's pickle factory. Combined, they provide a richly textured picture, and one that doesn't spare the olfactory system from less pleasant odors either, including garbage and decaying fish.

Total immersion in a good book can't be or replace the things that make life and travel so special—the unexpected conversations, the disasters that end in laughter, the friends you keep for ever—but it's a tiny escape without ever having to leave home.

READING ALOUD

People are often shy about reading aloud, either on their own or in front of others, and yet it's a liberating way to enjoy words.

- If you feel self-conscious, set aside a few minutes when no one else is around and begin with a small manageable bite from a book or poem that means something to you.

- You don't have to stand up to read aloud; you can curl up in an armchair just as easily.

- Pay attention to the shape of your mouth and the way that it moves to annunciate words clearly.

- Try recording yourself. Do you speak clearly? Or do your words slide into one another?

FRAME OF MIND

For your next read, consider choosing books to suit your mood. If you feel in need of a lift, pick titles that inspire warmth, joy, or happiness. If you need cheering, seek out a writer you know who can make you smile.

List the books that come to mind here:

➤ ....

....

➤ ....

....

➤ ....

....

➤ ....

....

➤ ....

....

SENSORY SENSATIONS

Here are just a few of the many titles that will lead you into other worlds:

Half of a Yellow Sun by Chimamanda Ngozi Adichie
The second novel from Nigerian author Chimamanda Ngozi Adichie takes you to Biafra, a state in West Africa that existed only between 1967 and 1970. Charting the life of three central characters amid Biafra's often overlooked struggle to remain independent and the violent civil war that ensued, Adichie uses local languages and evocative and unflinching sensory descriptions to take the reader to a place of intelligence, passion, and ultimately famine and destitution.

The Bastard of Istanbul by Elif Shafak
Telling the interwoven histories of two girls and their families, one Turkish, one Armenian-American, this novel is a vivid and colorful portrayal of the historic city. Each chapter is titled with a different food—orange peel, pomegranate seeds, dried figs—a nod to the sensory experience of visiting Istanbul.

The Wind-Up Bird Chronicle by Haruki Murakami
What starts out as a detective novel and becomes so much more, this Murakami novel takes the reader on a journey through Tokyo from the skyscraper buildings and the buzzing neon-lit Shinjuku district to the peace and calm of Imperial Gardens and the city's many tearooms.

Rebecca by Daphne du Maurier
The gothic manor house of Manderley with its overgrown rhododendrons makes an ideal backdrop for this classic suspense novel about a young woman whose surprise marriage to widower Maxim de Winter is overshadowed by the powerful presence of his late wife and all-too-alive and vicious housekeeper Mrs. Danvers. The rough seas and turbulent mists of the wild Cornish coast enhance the tale of foreboding, self-doubt, and untold secrets.

Captain Corelli's Mandolin by Louis de Bernières
Set on Cephalonia during the Italian and German occupation of World War Two, the beauty of this Ionian island and the strength of its people remain as the reality of war tries to tear it apart. Love—both platonic and romantic—is the core, but the Greek island is the star.

WORD BY WORD

Focus on the language used in the books that have moved you. Single out an individual word; look up unfamilar ones. Observe the rhythm of a sentence, a detail that conjures up a time or place.

List the words that you've noticed:

▷ ....
....

▷ ....
....

▷ ....
....

▷ ....
....

▷ ....
....

▷ ....
....

▷ ....
....

▷ ....
....

▷ ....
....

ONCE UPON A TIME

Record passages from books that transport you to another place.

Feel the Vibes

Can't escape the doldrums? Try raising your personal vibration.

"Everything in life is vibration," said physicist Albert Einstein. A vibration is a state of being, the energetic quality of a person, place, or thing. Everything in the universe is made of atoms that are vibrating at varying speeds—even in apparently solid things, such as rocks and wood. It makes sense that this vibration will vary from person to person—some people seem consistently "high vibe" or "low vibe"—as well as changing in the same individual depending on life events and their emotional state. Some days you will be in the flow and bright, at ease, and ready for anything. At the other end of the spectrum, among the lower vibrations, your mood might be heavy, dark, and out of sorts.

Sensing vibes is something most people do intuitively. When you meet someone for the first time, you may be attracted to their energy or decide to keep a distance. Late American psychiatrist David Hawkins even went so far as to create a scale categorizing the energy levels of emotions, ranging from zero to 1,000. He listed shame at 20, fear at 100, love at 500, and enlightenment at 700 and above. He put the energy level for courage at 200 and also made it the first level of empowerment, which included the willingness to stop blaming others and take responsibility for one's own feelings and actions.

LIFT YOUR ENERGY

How can you keep a check on personal vibes and know what helps you tune into a higher, happy zone? Here are seven ways to raise your vibrations . . .

1. Appreciate the Small Things

"Gratitude opens the door, the power, the wisdom, the creativity of the universe," says author Deepak Chopra. On an everyday level, gratitude is good for your vibrational health. Whether it's enjoying a cup of fresh, aromatic coffee, a brisk walk on a crisp fall day, or a hug with the loved one of your choice (whether human or animal), what's great in your life is worth being mindful about.

List five small things you feel grateful for.

2. Have a Boogie

By moving the body, the vibrations can start to shift as well, while sitting for too long can cause them to flatline. Rhythmic movement, such as dancing, especially combined with music, has a powerful influence and mood-enhancing effects on emotions. When you dance, your body releases endorphins (chemicals that reduce pain) and gets your cardiovascular system pumping. If you can't get to a class, dance at home: Even a 10-minute workout to your favorite music will get those vibrations moving in an upward spiral.

Choose your soundtrack. How do you want to feel? List songs that have moved you in the past, evoked happy memories, or transported you to a beautiful place.

3. Eat Yourself into a Higher Zone

If you believe food contains life-force energy, then feeding yourself on nutrient-dense foods will make you feel lighter, more vibrant, and alive. Think whole foods closest to their natural form—fruits and vegetables, nuts, seeds, and whole grains. Reduce lower-vibe energy items, such as fried or processed foods, and include lots of plant-based proteins.

For a more mindful mealtime, try the following:

- Set the table with your favorite tableware so you can look forward to the experience.
- Chew your food slowly—this will aid the digestive processes.
- Limit the amount of time you spend watching television while eating—your body and mind will thank you for it.

4. Meditate

The law of attraction says thoughts and belief systems send individual vibrations to the universe, which in turn responds by giving you a made-to-order set of experiences endorsing those thoughts and beliefs. One way to align with this law and remove obstacles that might be hampering the fulfillment of a dream or ambition is meditation. The practice can generate positive energy and help dispel low-vibrational emotions, such as anger, despair, shame, fear, and regret, while clearing the way for higher states, including joy and hope.

Why not give one of these meditations a try? Remember, it's normal for the mind to wander. Practice gently pulling it back to your meditation without judgment.

Open Awareness Meditation

- Set a timer for five to ten minutes, or longer if you choose.
- Find a comfortable place to sit.
- Allow your mind to freely traverse the landscape of your inner world and your senses: feelings, memories, sounds, smells, bodily sensations.
- Be receptive to whatever comes up. There is no right or wrong to this, no superior or inferior experiences. Be present to whatever is happening without getting caught up in it. You could think of it as just following a child a few steps behind, keeping them safe while they play unfettered.
- When the timer goes off, spend a moment paying attention to how you feel.

Reflect on your experience here.

....

....

....

....

....

....

....

....

Single Object, Experience, or Concept Meditation

- Set your timer for 5–10 minutes.
- Choose one of the following objects of focus and rest your mind there:

  Mantra—phrase or sound that you repeat over and over.

  Candle—focus your attention on its flickering flame.

  Visualization—picture a place or goal and explore the intricacies, creating as vivid and detailed a sensory experience as you can.

  Breath—follow its journey as it travels in and out of your body. Be curious about its sensations. Allow its rhythm to anchor you.

  Body scan—mentally scan from the very top of the head all the way to the tips of your toes. Pay attention to the sensations you find.

  Sound meditation—play a favorite track or piece of music, or attend or listen to a sound bath (an experience where instruments are played specifically for the purpose of immersing you in waves of sound).

- When the timer goes off, spend a moment paying attention to how you feel.

Reflect on your experience here.

....

....

....

....

....

....

....

....

....

....

....

....

5. Touch and Be Touched

One reason why primates touch each other is to ease group tensions in social situations. During physical touch or cuddling, the love hormone oxytocin is released, helping humans to feel connection and promoting a high-vibe sensation that contributes toward well-being and happiness. When touch comes as part of a massage, it can also rebalance hormones and reduce cortisol, the main stress hormone. Next time you're feeling low on energy or out of balance, find somewhere comfortable to sit and take a couple of deep breaths. As you exhale, screw your hands into a ball, hold, and release. Then begin.

- Turn both palms up and use one hand to support the other.

- Push the thumb of the bottom hand into the soft pads at the base of your hand and above your wrist.

- Apply whatever pressure is comfortable for you. Try to make it firm enough so that you feel it but gentle enough for it to be relaxing.

- Make firm circles with your thumb, as if you're smoothing your skin.

- Move onto the palm of the upper hand, circling and pushing out from the center of your palm across your hand. Notice the feeling of warmth that comes from the movement.

- Now focus on the pads at the bottom of each finger. Press into each one, circle, and note how that feels.

- Work your way from the bottom to the top of each finger on the upper hand. Imagine stretching the fingers out and give the tip of each one a squeeze when you get there.

- Finally, rub your hands together as if you're washing them. Slowly let them run over each other. Come to a stop, taking a deep breath and pausing to notice the calm.

- Repeat with the other hand.

6. Give—and Get Back

Have you ever been stingy with someone—with money, love, or time—and noticed how it brought down your mood? Meanness is said to lower the vibration. One way to counteract this is through generosity. Turning it around can work in your favor, too, so whatever you want more of in your life, try offering it to someone else. If you'd like to attract money, perhaps try giving some to charity. If you feel time-strapped, maybe set aside an hour to help someone else. If you feel you'd like to meet more people, why not say hello to a stranger?

What do you want more of in your life?

....

....

....

....

....

....

....

....

....

....

....

....

....

....

....

7. Open Your Heart

Love is one of the highest vibrating states so no wonder it's the subject of myriad books, movies, artworks, and wise sayings—not least "love makes the world go round." And "love always raises your vibration," says reiki master Torsten A. Lange. Tune into this energy and feel the benefit. This also includes self-love. Listen to your heart, do what you truly love, and be true to the real you.

Bring to mind someone who's easy to love, center their image in your heart, and imagine them sitting with you. Do you detect a sense of joy and happiness, possibly a light and expanded feeling? Does the feeling lift you up? How do you feel?

Easy Does It

*Freeze-frame a situation and find a new way
to have a nice time.*

Plane missed. Bag stolen. Luggage lost. When faced with something completely out of your control, have you ever found yourself in shock laughter at how you ended up there? When you're on the road, things can—and do—go wrong all the time. But it's possible to turn these misadventures into a wider philosophy on life, one to help you through stressful situations and come out smiling or, at the very least, no worse off than before. Called the "having-a-nice-time" philosophy, it's all about embracing the power of freeze-framing and easy wins.

It isn't a philosophy for life-changing events such as bereavement or chronic mental or physical illness. Rather, it's meant to apply to life's everyday hiccups, challenges, and misfortunes. It allows you to stop and reflect on the moment as it's happening and reframe it into something more palatable. Even better, it can also be used as a tool to tune in and fully appreciate when things unexpectedly go your way, whether that's finding $20 in your suitcase or securing a table at a much-garlanded eatery after a last-minute cancellation. It's important to note and celebrate these positive moments because they're the easiest wins of all.

So let's return to those negative zones and see how a having-a-nice-time philosophy can help to view them in a different light. While you can't turn a terrible situation into the best day of your life, often you can seize back an element of control. How? There are three elements.

TIME TO TAKE BACK CONTROL

Learn to put the "having-a-nice-time" philosophy into action:

1. Freeze-frame the Scene and Readjust Your Reaction

When you're faced with a stressful situation, the first thing to do is stop, take a moment to breathe, and readjust your mindset into a more positive space. Tools that can help with this include:

- Employing dark humor to speculate just how badly things could have turned out.
- Finding the silver lining even if (and almost especially if) it's a real stretch and involves scraping a very deep barrel.
- Not worrying about small things over which you have no control—doing so is surely time wasted.

2. Have Yourself a Nice Time

Mindset suitably readjusted, it's time to explore the second part of the having-a nice-time philosophy: how you can still have a nice time. It may sound flippant, but if the worst has already happened, why add fuel to the fire? For many, the initial impulse is to seek out who or what is responsible for the problem, expending precious time and energy in the process. They might then try to achieve total resolution, compensation, or even an improvement on the previous status quo. There's nothing intrinsically wrong with any of this—compensation and problem-solving is often appropriate. However, sometimes a return to the status quo or to the expected just isn't possible and trying to get there can be both arduous and destructive.

And why do we want to just have a "nice time?" Why not have a "great time" or a "fulfilling time?" You want to set yourself up for a really easy win. Fewer, more achievable goals mean a faster road to reaching them. It's about not trying too hard, or having unachievable expectations. Life is hard enough, give yourself a break. Set a reasonable goal, and when you achieve it, celebrate it in a way that suits you.

Imagine you're on a road trip and have just driven seven hours in the wrong direction. Rather than pushing to make up lost time or thinking your trip is ruined, you might be able to turn it into the most enjoyable day of the whole trip by stopping at every roadside attraction that catches your eye.

The having-a-nice-time philosophy isn't rocket science, but it's a way of thinking that's easily forgotten when you're stressed. Remember that you can freeze-frame a challenging situation, take a look around, and appreciate it for what it is—a good story that you have the power to influence.

3. Use Humor to Cope

Never underestimate the power of humor. While you don't have to aim for becoming a stand-up comedian, making yourself laugh about feeling uncomfortable or irritated is a useful coping mechanism.

"The human race has one really effective weapon, and that is laughter."

Mark Twain

THE LAST LAUGH

Bring to mind the last time you experienced a stressful moment. Can you find
something funny or absurd about the situation? Write it down here and read
it often. Laughing can make you feel more positive about getting through
something awkward.

....

....

....

....

....

....

....

....

....

....

....

....

....

....

....

....

Break Free From the Past

Identifying and understanding the origins of emotional triggers can provide an opportunity to stop running from past hurts and reclaim control over unconscious reactions.

Have you ever found yourself in the grip of a sudden and powerful emotion because of something someone said or did, or maybe just because of a look they gave you? Whether it was anger, fear, or jealousy, whatever overwhelmed you caused you to react in a way that felt out of character, perhaps even irrational. Once the feeling subsided, you might have looked back bewildered, wondering what on earth came over you, and then perhaps felt embarrassed about your behavior. If this sounds familiar, you may have experienced a reaction to an emotional trigger.

What Is an Emotional Trigger?

An external factor that prompts a subconscious negative thought or belief that, in most cases, has its roots in the past. In other words, it's a reminder of an old hurt that's never healed. Early exposure to criticism and hurtful comments or conflict and trauma can create deep-seated wounds. As children start to experience a world that isn't always kind, they develop a learned response designed to protect these wounds and themselves from further pain.

Growing up with overly critical parents, for example, might make a person bridle at any form of criticism as an adult. Likewise, having caregivers who constantly argued might lead someone to avoid all conflict later in life. If the emotional wounds are not addressed and healed at the time of the initial hurt, they might be buried or unrecognized. When an event or a person comes along and unintentionally scratches the wound, that past pain is set off and flares up. Not recognizing or being sensitive to emotional triggers is one of the most common causes of relationship conflict.

Why Do We Have Emotional Triggers?

The brain is hardwired to protect you by constantly scanning for cues that signal danger, which, when detected, stimulates powerful emotions such as fear or anger. This prepares the body to overcome the threat—as seen in the fight, flight, or freeze response. One of our most powerful subconscious fears is being rejected. In primitive times, rejection—or exclusion from the community—meant vulnerability to predators and an increased risk of death. There was safety in numbers. To this day, the human brain remains vigilant to cues that signal rejection. The problem arises when the brain misinterprets otherwise nonthreatening facial expressions, words, or tones of voice by linking them to past pain.

Say, for example, you find yourself in a team meeting and your boss praises individual members but for some reason doesn't mention you. Though, at a rational level, you know they value you and your contribution, you feel angry. Go below the surface of the emotion and you might discover you feel hurt and excluded. If you go even deeper, the reaction might, for example, be linked to an incident at school when a teacher praised your friend for a project on which you both collaborated, but ignored your contribution. This might have left you feeling unacknowledged, invisible, and insignificant. In this situation, it's easy to blame your boss for not valuing you—or even to accuse them of favoritism—when it might not be the case.

When you're emotionally triggered, neither the situation nor the people prompting the response in the present are the likely cause. Rather, the clue to unraveling what's going on lies within yourself. In the words of writer Anaïs Nin: "We don't see things as they are, we see things as we are."

However, this also creates an opportunity. By recognizing what's happened when the trigger occurs, there's potential to explore where it's come from and to try to identify the original wound. This can be done by adopting a spirit of curiosity aimed at untangling the intricate pattern of thought, feeling, and behavior associated with the trigger.

What Makes Up a Trigger?

If we were to look at the basic pattern of an emotional trigger response, it would follow a TTFB pattern: a *trigger* leads to a *thought* that goes to a *feeling*, resulting in a *behavior*. The cycle then repeats with the behavior leading to another thought and feeling, and so it continues. This is called a looping thought pattern. Just as there are behavioral habits like nail biting or smoking, a person can develop automatic emotional habits they might prefer not to have.

These habits can be altered. The first step involves identifying and naming the trigger, then creating new ways of responding and behaving that match a different version of ourselves. Because many automatic emotional responses often involve feelings of embarrassment, shame, or guilt, one way to disempower triggers and heal wounds is to practice self-compassion. It's easy to be self-critical and judge harshly, believing you need to be more in control of yourself and your behavior. But just as you wouldn't expect someone to walk properly on a broken leg, how can you expect yourself to interact when there are unhealed emotional wounds? Extensive studies show that people who practice self-compassion have increased feelings of happiness and connectedness, as well as decreased anxiety, depression, and fear of failure. It's associated with being more comfortable to admit mistakes, less self-criticism, and a greater desire to change what might be unhelpful behaviors. It's also been shown to reduce a person's sensitivity to emotional triggers.

What's Self-compassion?

Self-compassion involves being kind to yourself when you perceive your behavior to have fallen short of your own expectations, acknowledging everyone makes mistakes, as well as realizing no one's perfect and it's completely natural to feel this way. By sitting with uncomfortable feelings and accepting rather than judging them harshly, it's possible to achieve a renewed sense of perspective and balance.

A phenomenal sense of safety and release can accompany the recognition of emotional triggers and realization that they can be controlled. Relationship patterns can be seen in a new light, with destructive ones of blame and conflict broken. An attitude of curiosity and self-compassion can neutralize emotional triggers and allow relationships to grow deeper and stronger.

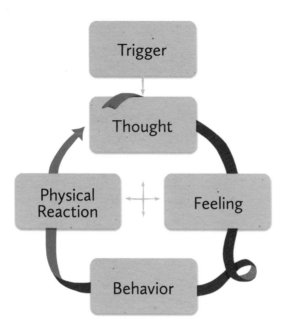

TAKE BACK CONTROL

Too often you speak to yourself with words you would never say to a friend, often without realizing it. By paying attention to your self-talk, you can change the message and how you say it. Your inner voice is yours and you can exert your control over it. Use it not as critic but as motivator. Be your own best friend.

Think for a moment about the occasions you talk to yourself. What tone does your inner voice use most often? Is it friendly and encouraging? Or is your inner voice your inner critic, making harsh comments?

List some of the words and phrases you use here.

▶ ....

....

▶ ....

....

▶ ....

....

HEAL AN EMOTIONAL TRIGGER

Identify the Emotional Trigger

Ask yourself which negative patterns of behavior you tend to repeat and what the trigger usually is. Note them here.

Example: *"When I'm out with my partner, I get upset if they talk to someone and seem more interested in them than me."*

....

....

....

....

....

....

What Looping Thought Pattern Occurs as a Result?

What initial thought follows the trigger? What's the resulting feeling and then finally how do you behave?

Example: *"I think they must find the other person really attractive, which makes me feel hurt and rejected. I then accuse my partner of flirting and we end up having an argument."*

....

....

....

....

....

....

Break the Loop

Look at your looping thought pattern and ask yourself how you could think, feel, and act differently. How would your preferred version of yourself think, feel, and act?

Example: *"I know I am feeling jealous, but I don't have to act on it."*

....

....

....

....

....

....

Close your eyes and practice visualizing yourself experiencing better thoughts, feelings, and behaviors. Practice this visualization daily.

Exercise Self-compassion

Take a minute to remind yourself that no one is perfect. How could you be kinder to yourself when you're in the grip of an emotional trigger? What could you say to yourself that shows compassion toward the hurt you're feeling? Make a list of ways that you can comfort yourself.

Example: *"Spend time with my partner in ways that make me feel more secure about our relationship—talking with me about my work; cooking a meal together; going for a walk in the park."*

....

....

....

....

....

....

Hidden Depths

Challenging yourself to try new things is usually beneficial, but there can be advantages to staying within your comfort zone.

Sometimes it can feel as though life is one endless swirl of positive advice, upbeat hashtags, calls to action, and encouraging suggestions. In the pursuit of a happier, more fulfilled life, many exhortations center on pushing limits and challenging boundaries. The thinking seems to be that only when freed from one's own limitations can someone truly experience what they're capable of.

There are times when this is sound advice, as previous pages in this journal attest. Overcoming the negative self-talk that's stopping you from submitting a job application, pushing yourself past nervousness to join a new club, or squashing down shyness to strike up a conversation with someone at a party—these are all ways in which forcing yourself past your own personal safety net can be positive, even enriching. Yet there's also a strength and sense of achievement that comes from knowing what's right for you and what makes you feel content. After all, what are comfort zones for, if not to protect us?

Embracing Your Safe Space

If pushing yourself has a negative impact on other aspects of your life, perhaps it's worth reassessing how valuable this exertion is. Consider a high-flying career that demands blood, sweat, tears, as well as time away from family, friends, and leisure time. As admirable, even enviable, as it may look, is it always worth it? If someone has a passion and talent for art and commits their time, energy, and resources to being the best they can be at it, rather than diversifying into, say, karate—they might still be within their comfort zone, but in a way that's positive.

Expanding your horizons, accepting challenges, and being proud of hard-won achievements—these are all components of what makes you exceptional. But you are no less exceptional if you drain the cup of life within the perimeters of your comfort zone. Depth, not width. Comfort zones are no less fertile breeding zones for achievement, fulfillment, and excitement than are danger zones.

EMBRACING YOUR LIMITATIONS

Letting go of what you wish or hope for and accepting what is can be a painful process. Yet it's only by working with what you have that you open yourself up to what is possible.

1. Try Not To Skip Ahead

Living too much in the future or past—becoming too attached to outcomes—often means missing out on the present moment. Have you ever pictured the outcome of a project or imagined finishing something before you've even begun? Record any times that come to mind here.

2. Opportunity Knocks

When life doesn't follow the path you'd expected, it's possible that new, more authentic directions will present themselves. It's about viewing limitations as an opportunity. Is there a challenge or limitation that you are facing? How might you view it in a different way?

....

....

....

....

....

....

....

....

....

....

....

....

....

....

....

....

....

FREE YOUR MINDSET

It's possible to reframe obstacles or limitations and turn them into strengths.

- Think of something you want to achieve.

- Now think of all the obstacles that are getting in the way of you achieving it.

- Go through each obstacle, one by one, and reframe it by assigning it an action. For example, perhaps your lack of knowledge is an obstacle. What action could you take that would turn this into a strength? How about seeking out a learning opportunity? And documenting your progress?

- Everyone has limitations. What defines your life is how you react to them, and that's something that you can control. What will you turn your limitations into?

"To know fully even one field or one land is a lifetime's experience. In the world of poetic experience it is depth that counts, not width."

Patrick Kavanagh

STERLING
New York

An Imprint of Sterling Publishing Co., Inc.

ISBN 978-1-4549-4401-0

Distributed in Canada by Sterling Publishing Co., Inc.
c/o Canadian Manda Group, 664 Annette Street
Toronto, Ontario M6S 2C8, Canada

For information about custom editions, special sales, and premium and corporate
purchases, please contact Sterling Special Sales at 800-805-5489 or
specialsales@sterlingpublishing.com.

Manufactured in Singapore

2 4 6 8 10 9 7 5 3 1

sterlingpublishing.com

Editorial: Susie Duff, Catherine Kielthy, Jane Roe
Design by Jo Chapman
Publisher: Jonathan Grogan

Words credits: Elizabeth Bennett, Alex Bowers, Fi Darby, Ruby Deevoy, Kerry Dolan,
Beverley D'Silva, Donna Findlay, Laura Gabrielle Feasey, Egle Grigaliunaite, Katy Holbird,
Stephanie Lam, Adele Little Caemmerer, Emma Newlyn, Isabel Norman-Butler,
Dawn Quest, Wendy Pratt, Sarah Rodrigues, Fiona Symington-Mitchell

Illustrations: Ruth Allen, Holly Astle, Louise Billyard, Katherine Buchanan,
Cat Finnie, Claire van Heukelom, Lylean Lee, Amy Leonard, Sophie Minto,
Irina Perju, Seeta Roy, Silvia Stecher, Sara Thielker, Katie Tomlinson,
Michelle Urra, Kimberley Laura Walker, Thomas White
Cover illustration: Sophie Minto